FINDING the LIGHT

Story and Art by Bobbi Dooley Hunter

Written and Illustrated by Bobbi Dooley Hunter

Published by Bobbi Dooley Hunter
Santa Ynez, California

ISBN: 979-8-9857568-1-4

Light of the Moon, Inc.
Partnering with self-published authors since 2009
Book Design/Production/Consulting
Carbondale, Colorado • www.lightofthemooninc.com

Dedication

This book is dedicated to my family,
as it was they who made Sensorio happen!
Grandad introduced us to the land many years ago.
Ken had vision to see the unique potential for the valley.
Seth encouraged us in our dreams and endeavors.
Cameron was the liaison from the beginning of Sensorio's production,
working towards the finished product and helping me polish this book.
Our grandchildren loved the story of how we found the light, hence this book!

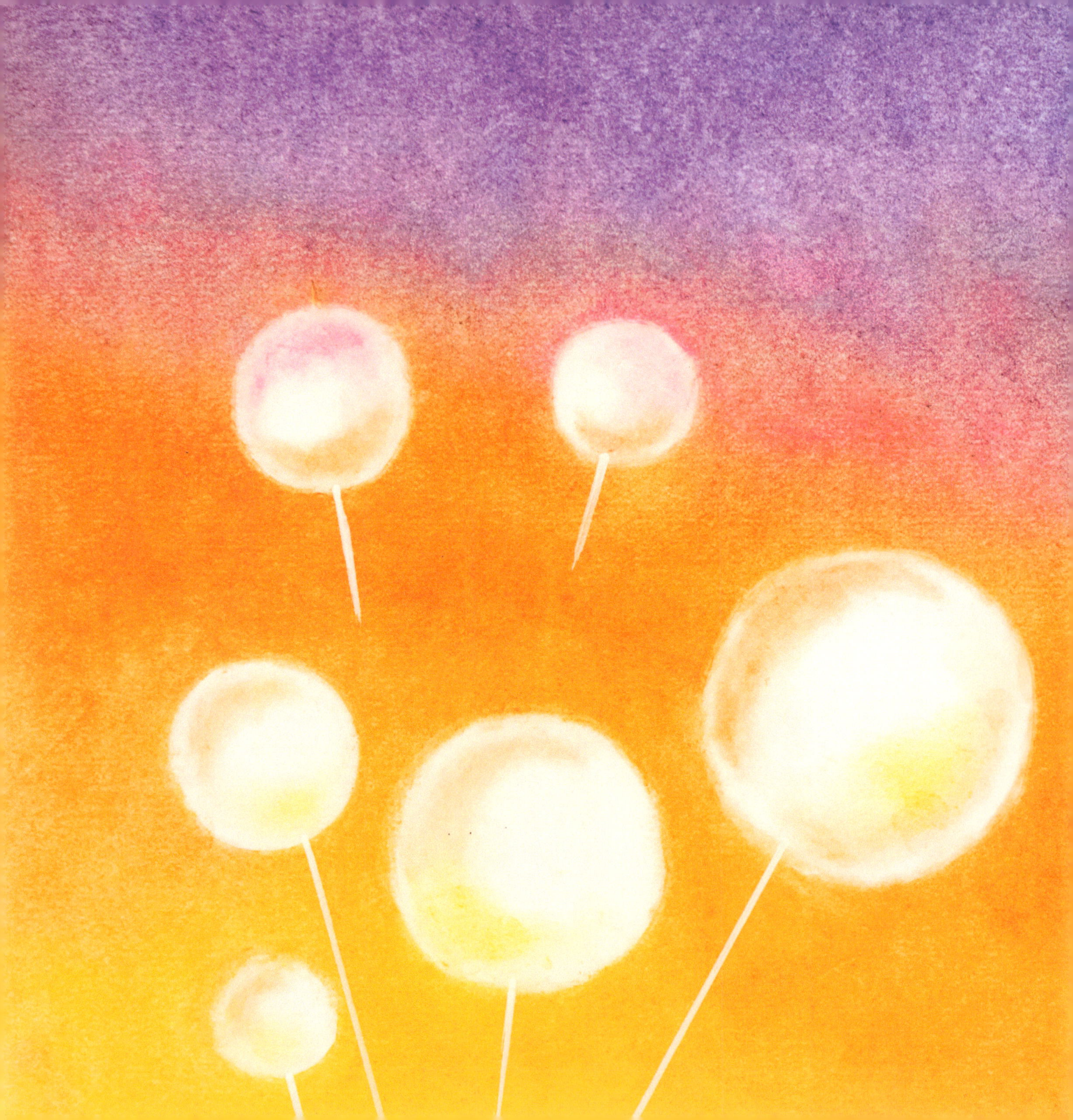

Preface

Sensorio is a large-scale art installation and sensory experience for entertainment, exploration, meditation, and adventure located in central California, near the town of Paso Robles. For years, my husband and I wanted to create a space for people to enjoy as they walked through these valleys of ancient oak trees and golden light, but were unsure of our direction. In 2017, we traveled through Australia and came upon Uluru in the center of the country. Bruce Munro, an artist from England, had installed a 'Field of Light' at the base of the red mountain. There were thousands of white balls on long stems we could walk amongst on meandering boardwalks. As dusk fell, the white balls and stems turned every color of the rainbow and waved in the breeze. It was quite spectacular on the desert floor! We were in awe of the site. We contacted Bruce Munro upon our return to California. He visited us at Sensorio, and we decided to install a Field of Light in a beautiful twisting valley. This book is about our journey.

Come visit us at SENSORIO... www.sensoriopaso.com

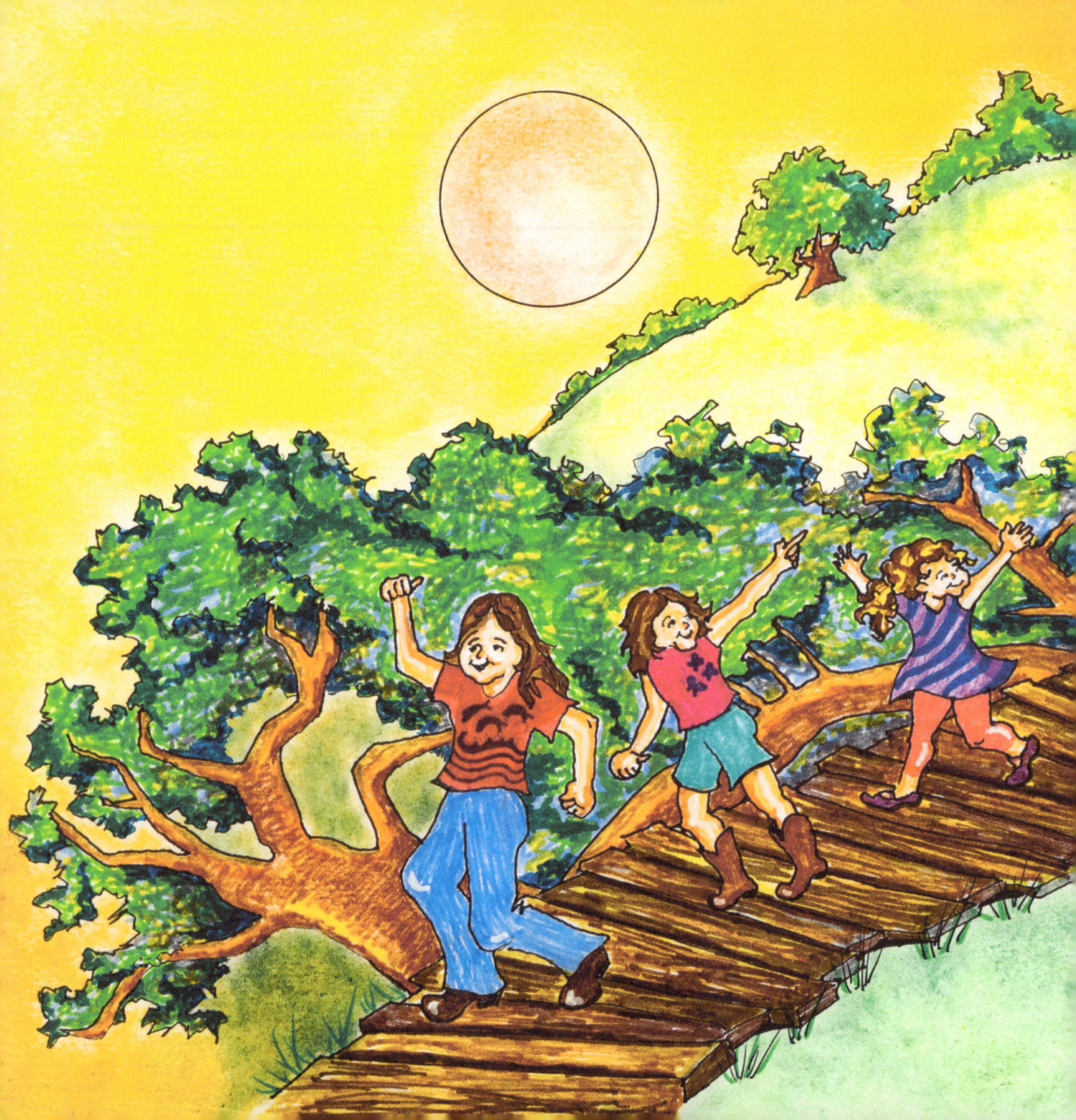

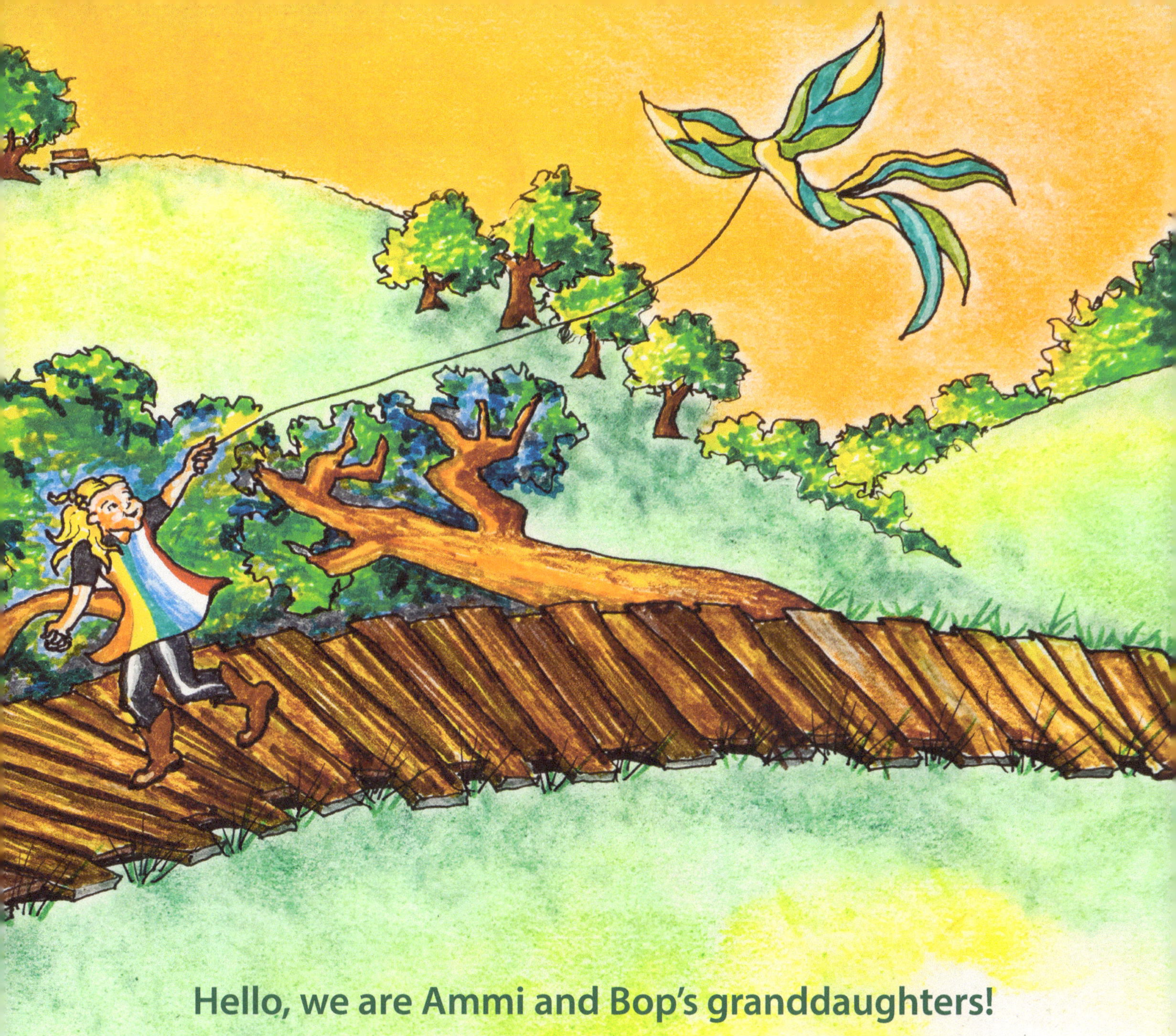

Hello, we are Ammi and Bop's granddaughters!

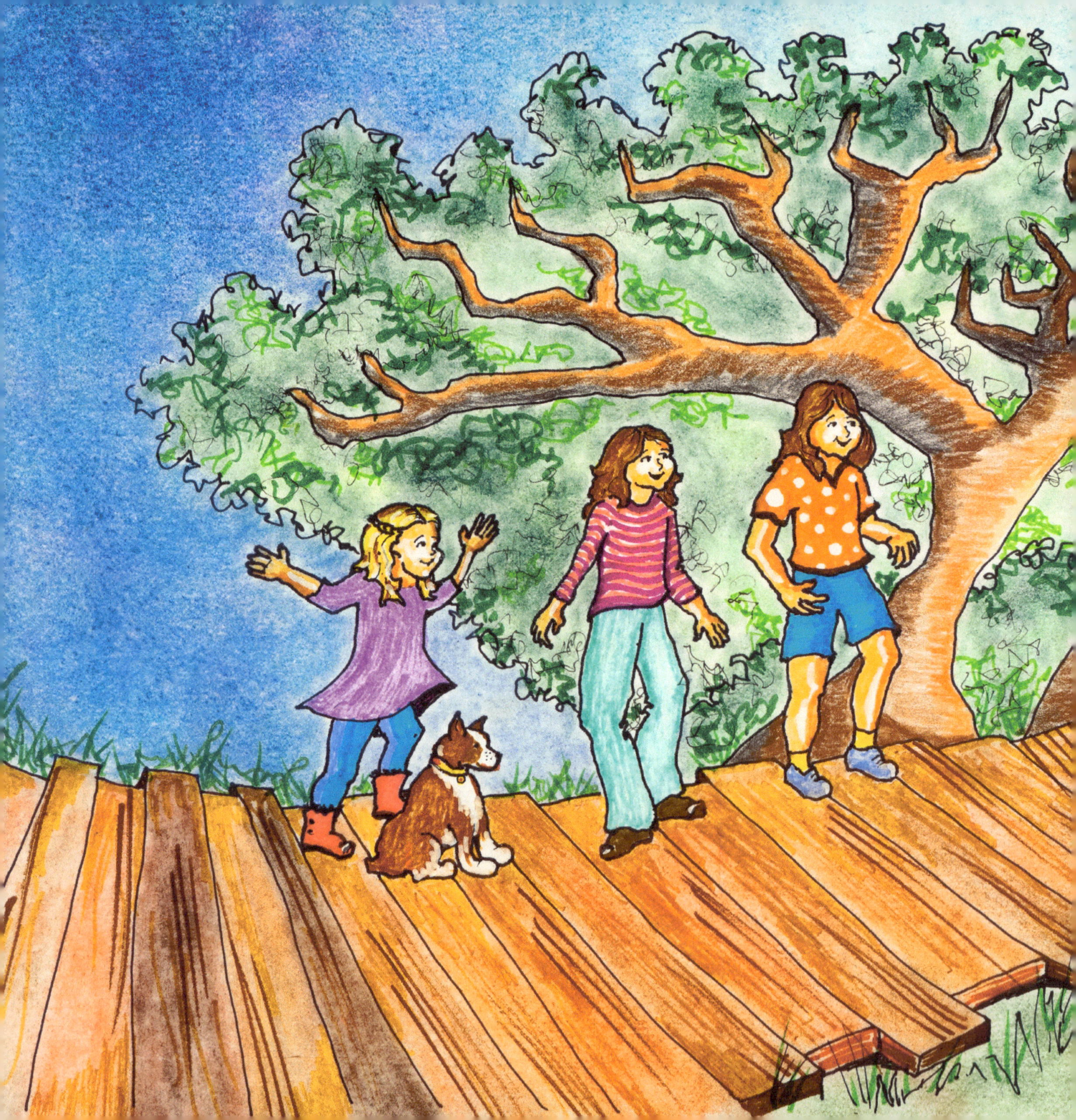

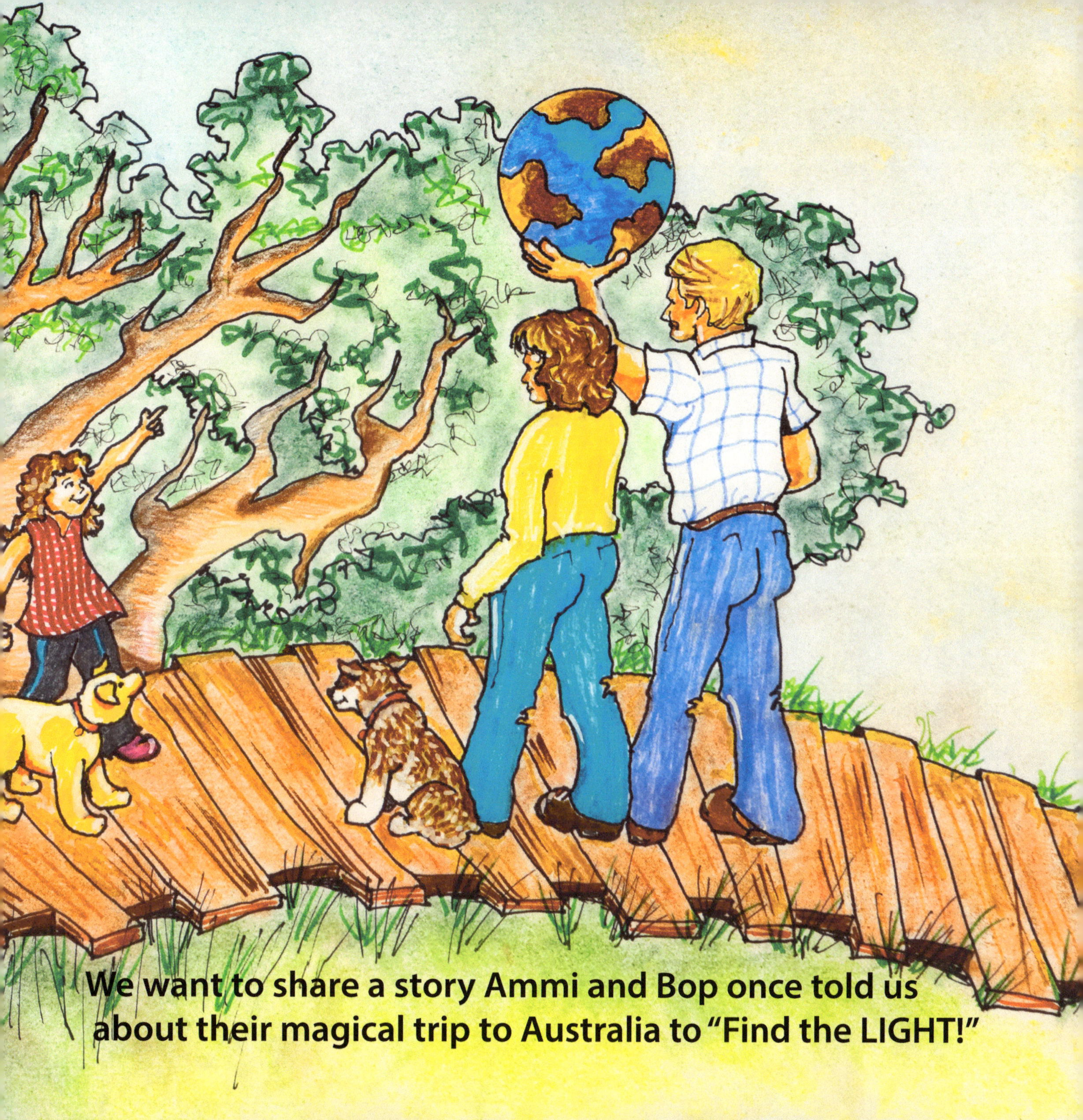

We want to share a story Ammi and Bop once told us about their magical trip to Australia to "Find the LIGHT!"

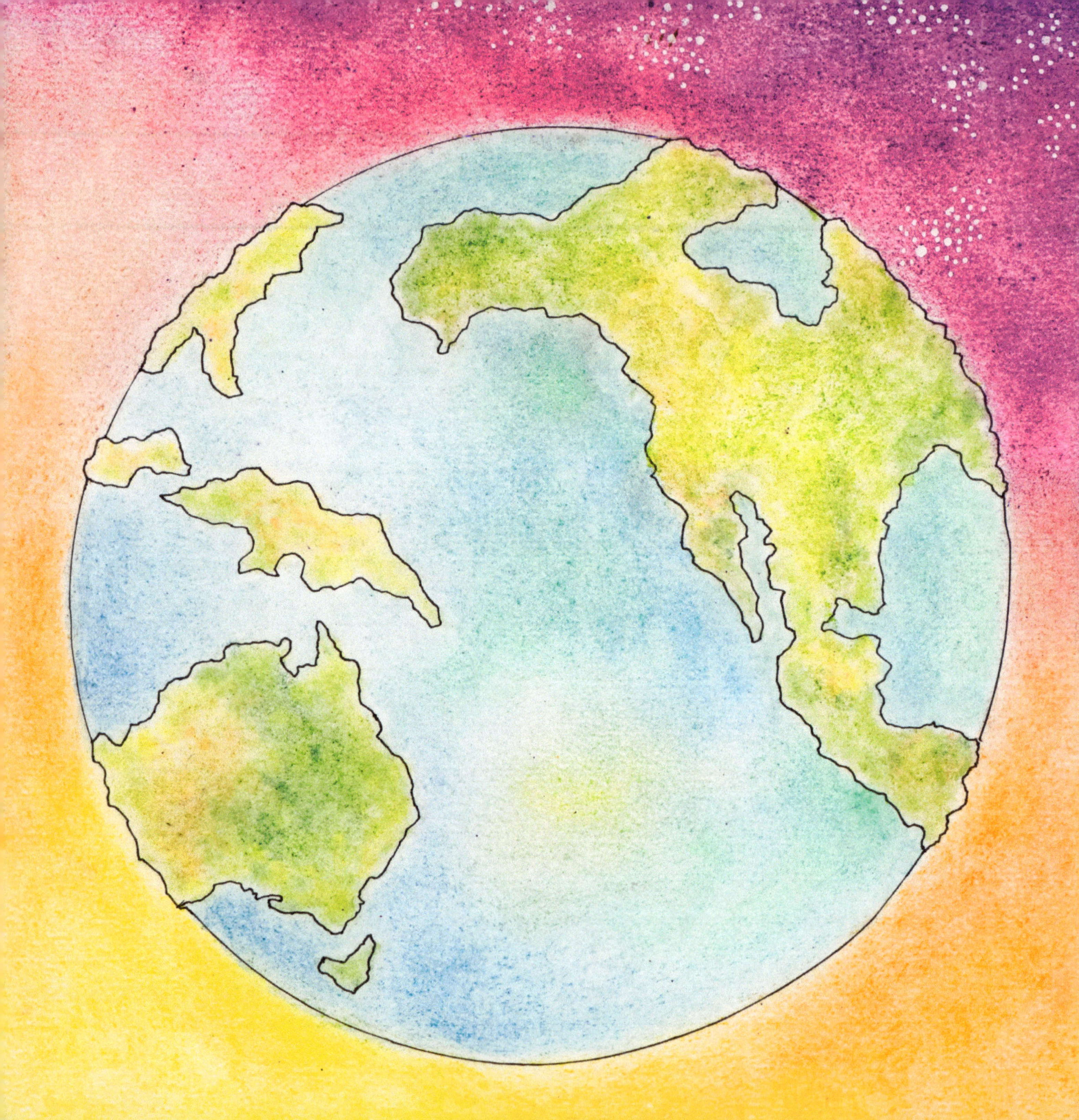

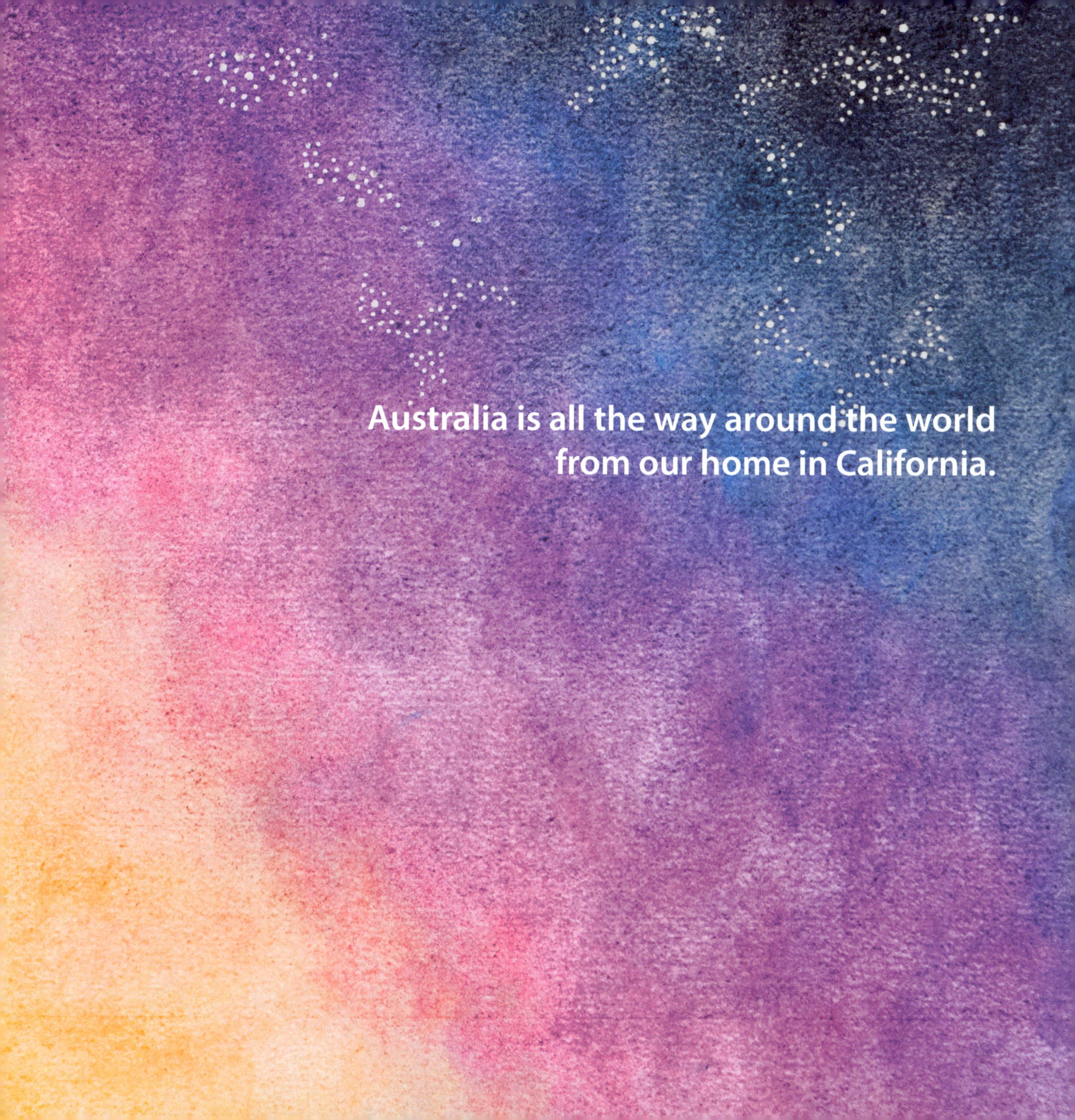

Australia is all the way around the world
from our home in California.

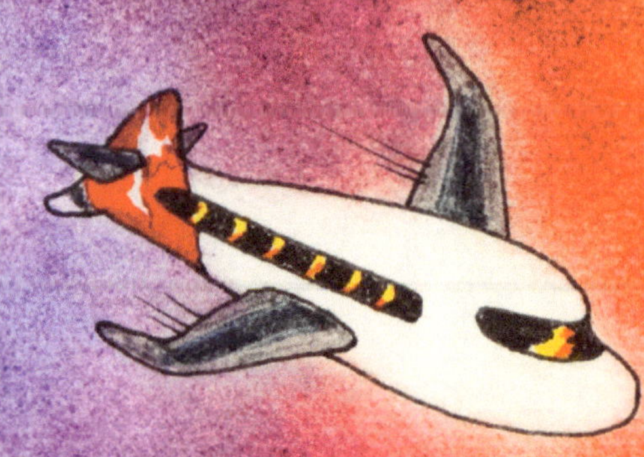

Ammi and Bop got on an airplane and flew into the heart of Australia, to a place called Uluru (oo-loo-roo).

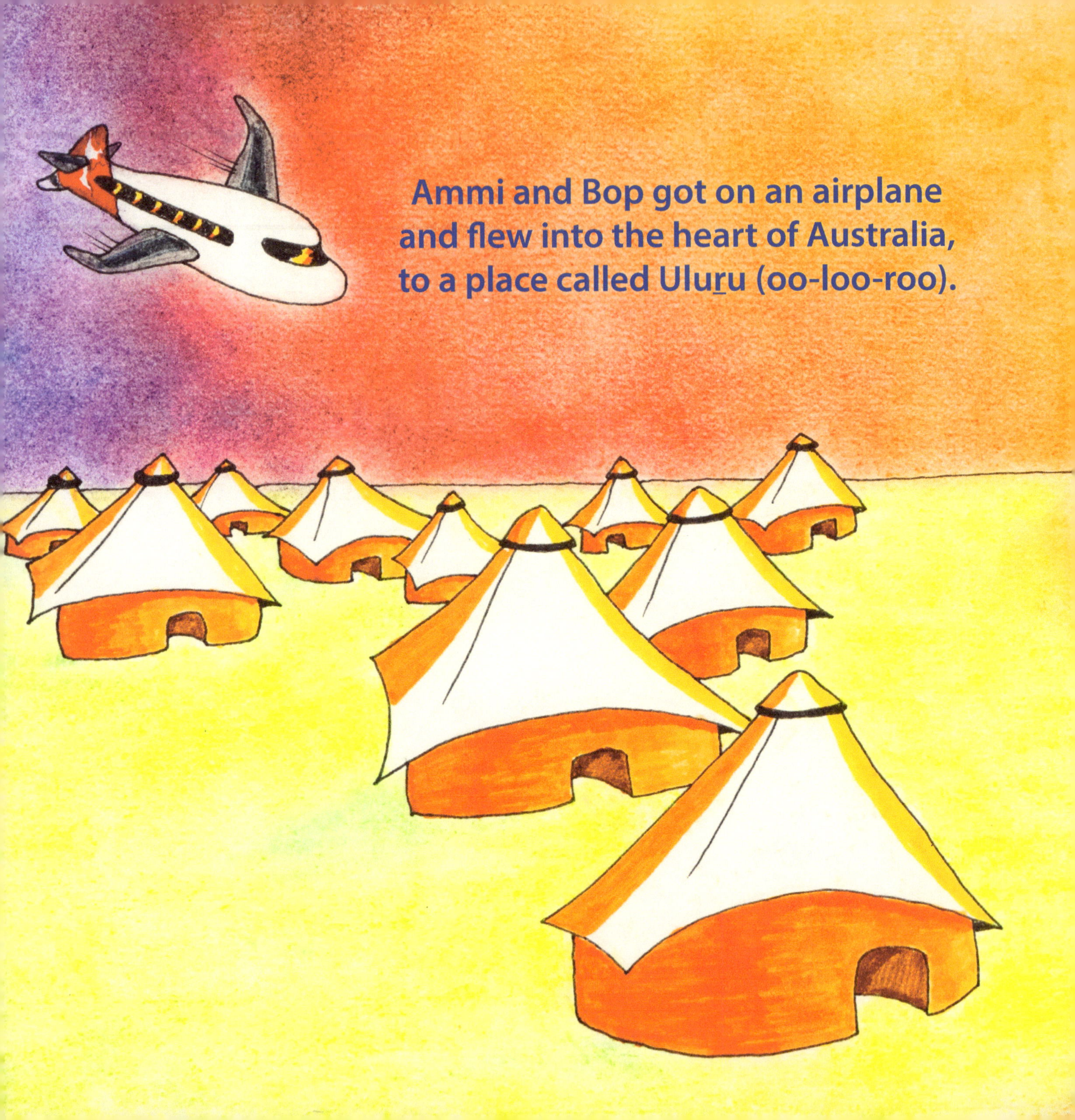

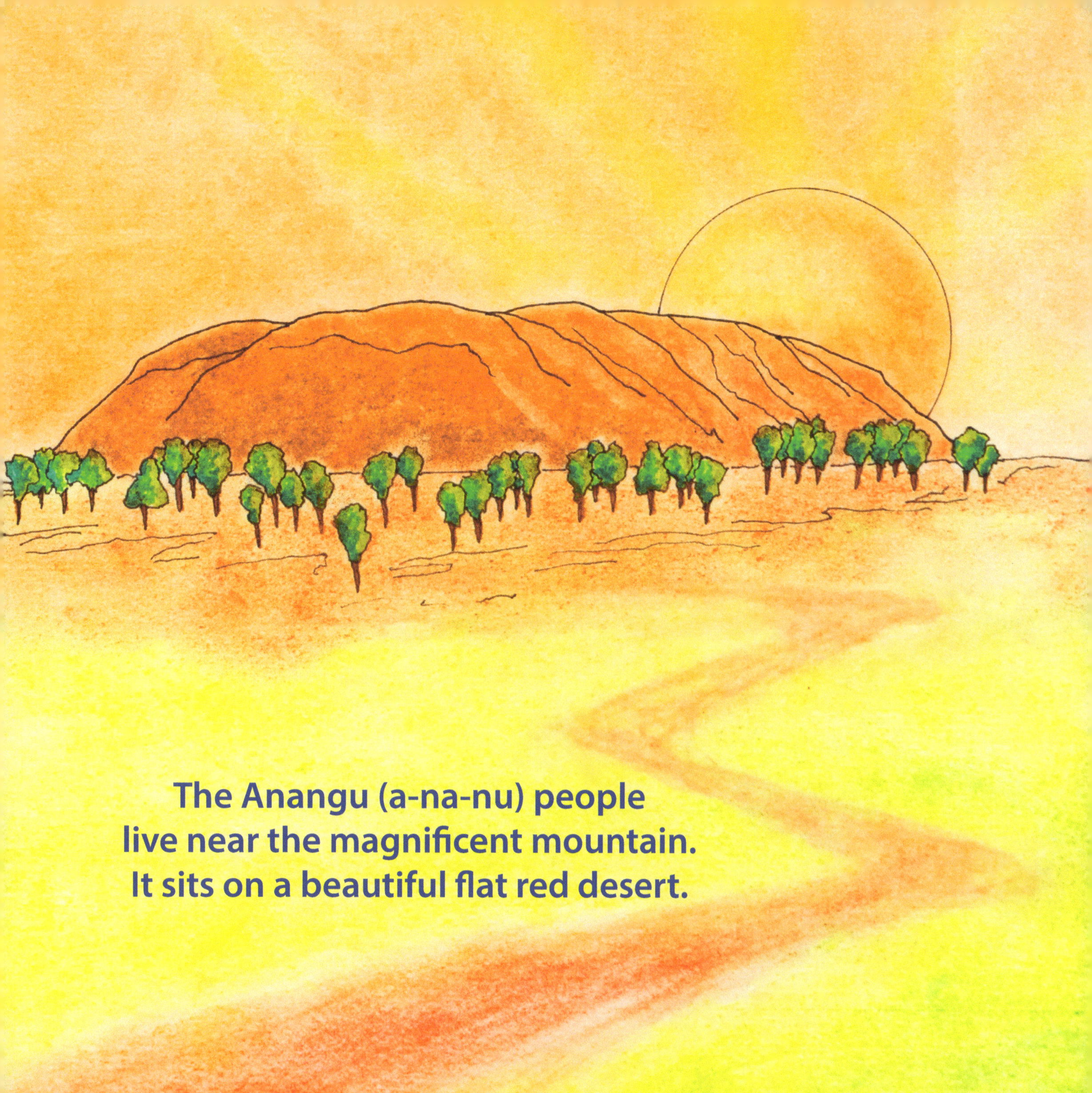

The Anangu (a-na-nu) people
live near the magnificent mountain.
It sits on a beautiful flat red desert.

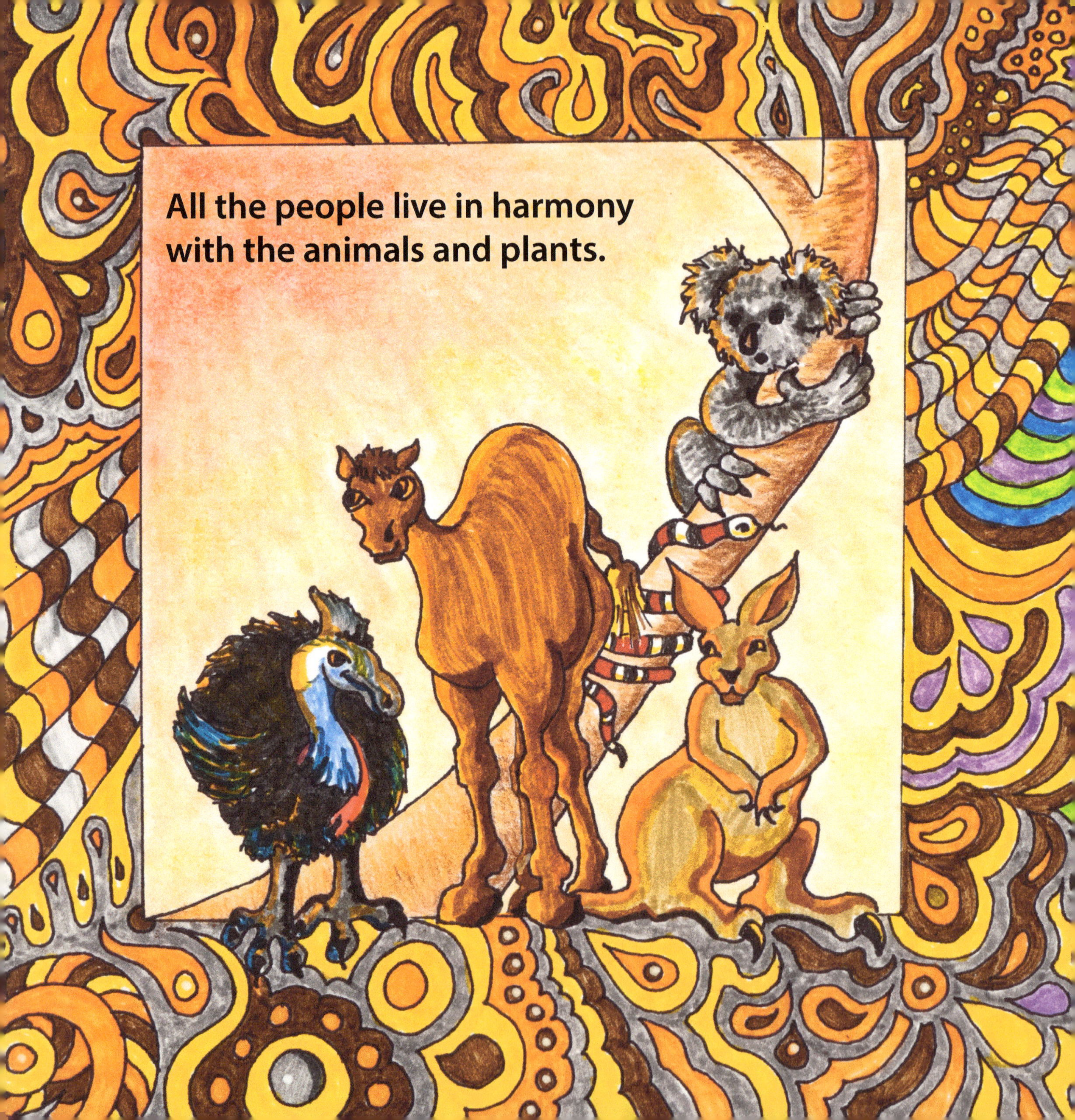
All the people live in harmony
with the animals and plants.

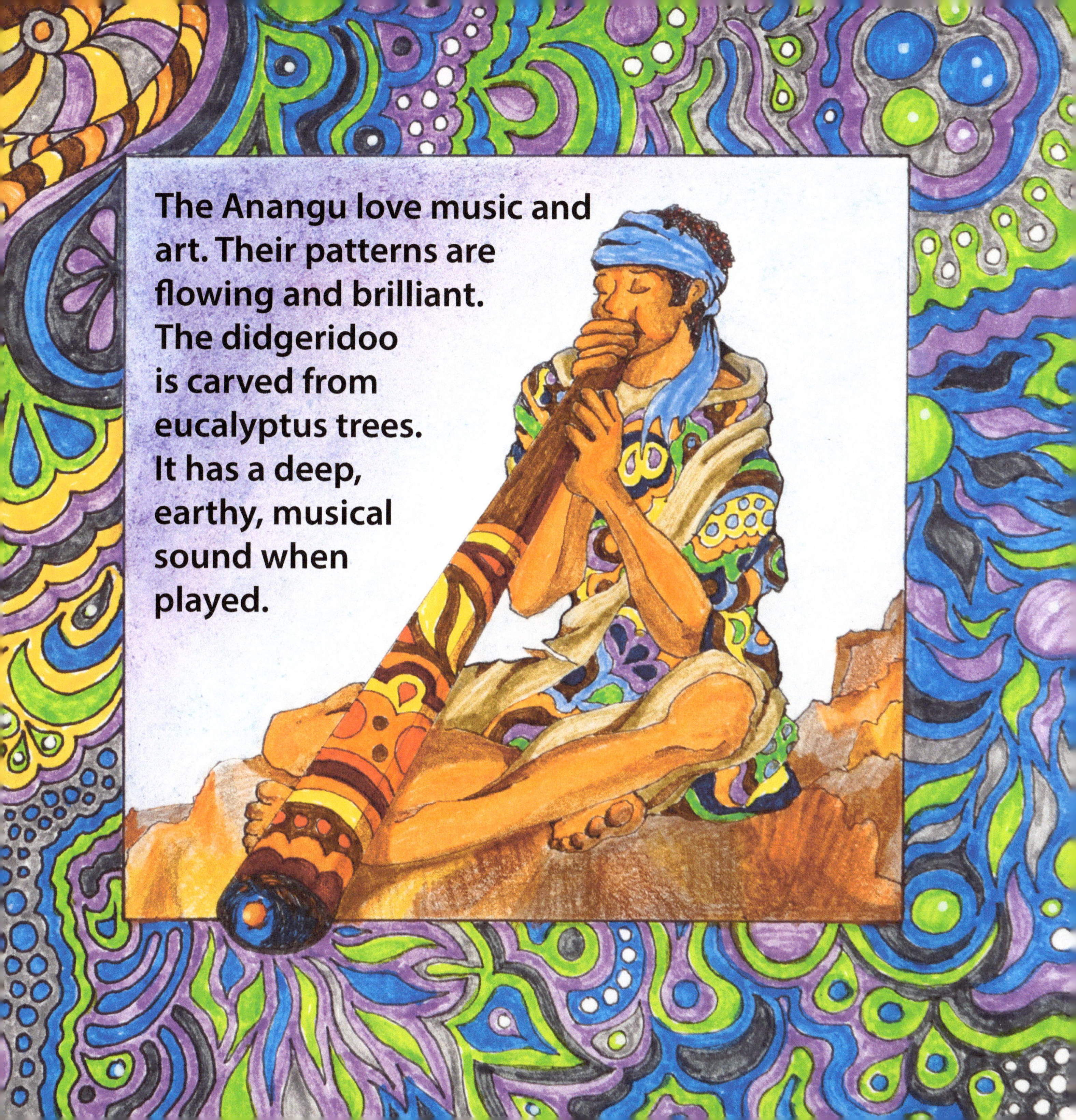

The Anangu love music and art. Their patterns are flowing and brilliant. The didgeridoo is carved from eucalyptus trees. It has a deep, earthy, musical sound when played.

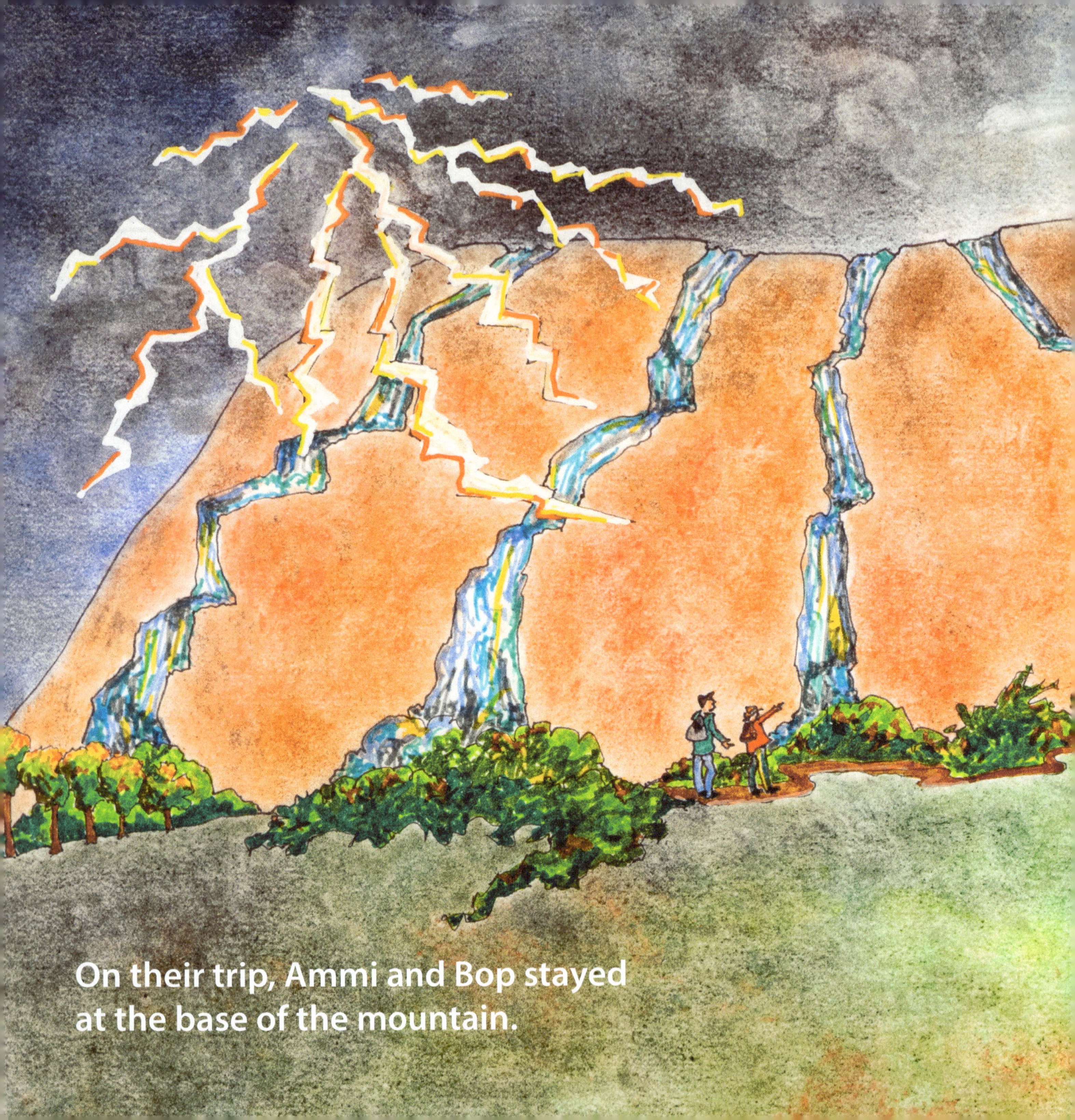
On their trip, Ammi and Bop stayed
at the base of the mountain.

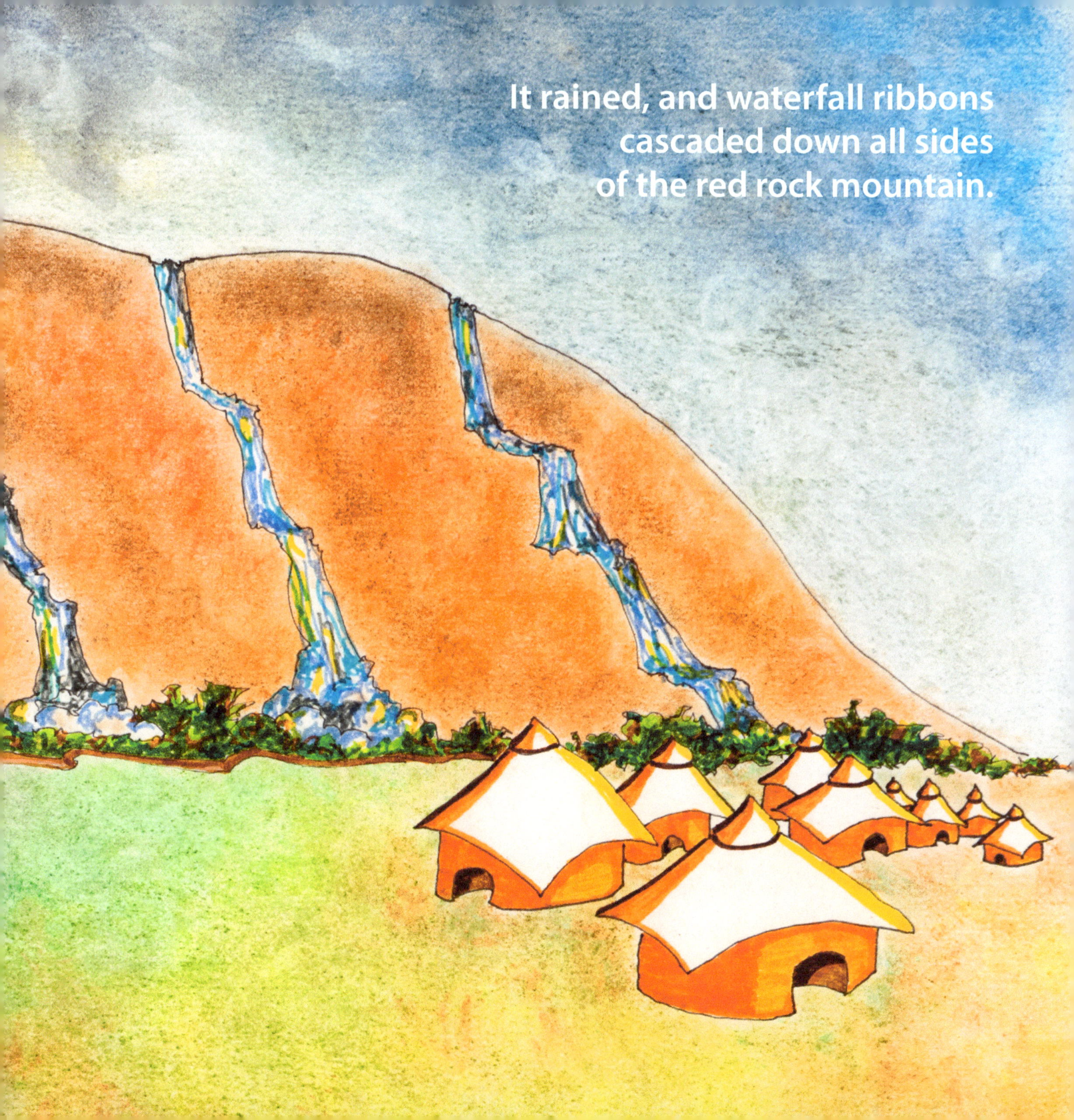
It rained, and waterfall ribbons
cascaded down all sides
of the red rock mountain.

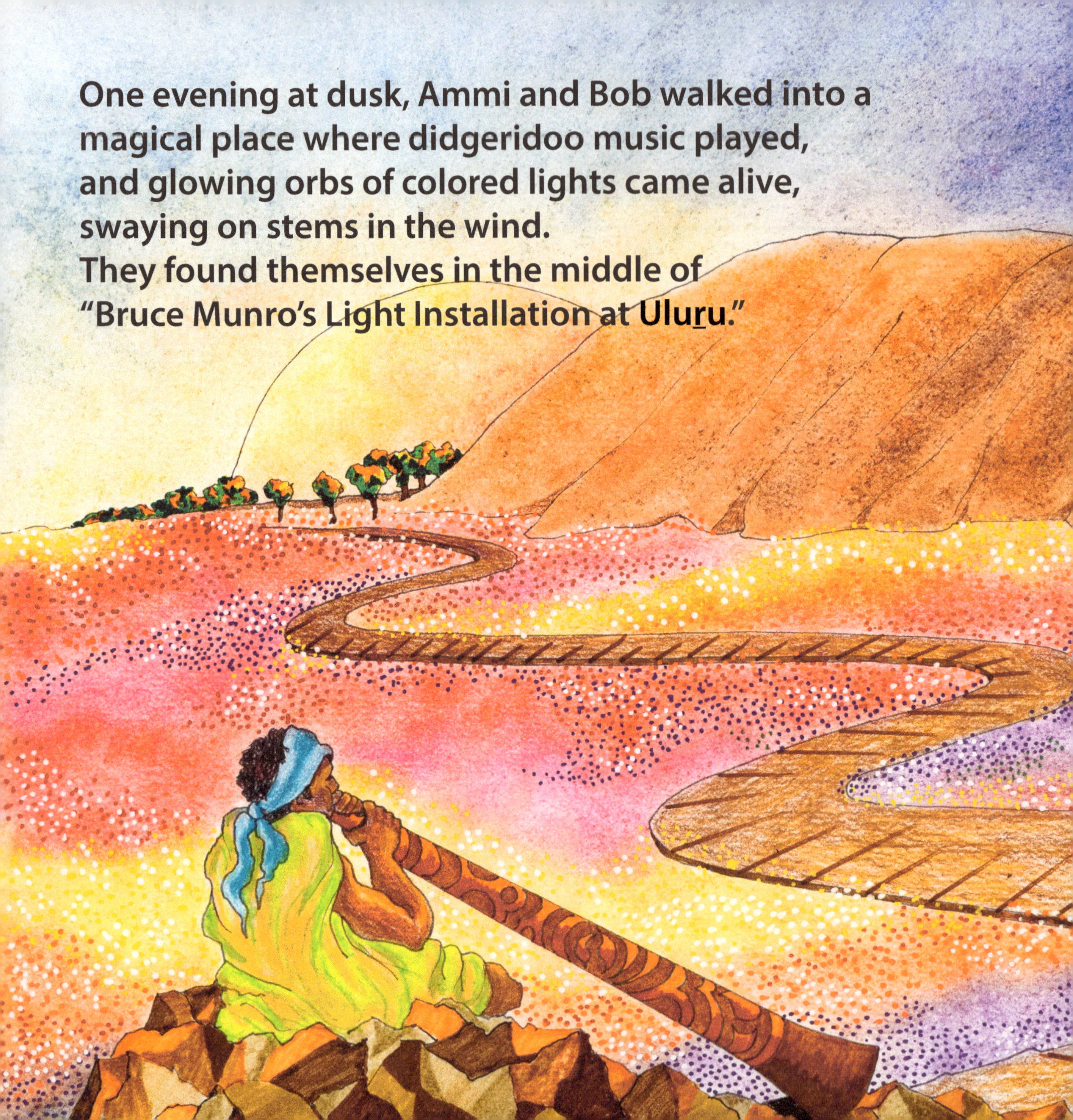

One evening at dusk, Ammi and Bob walked into a
magical place where didgeridoo music played,
and glowing orbs of colored lights came alive,
swaying on stems in the wind.
They found themselves in the middle of
"Bruce Munro's Light Installation at Uluru."

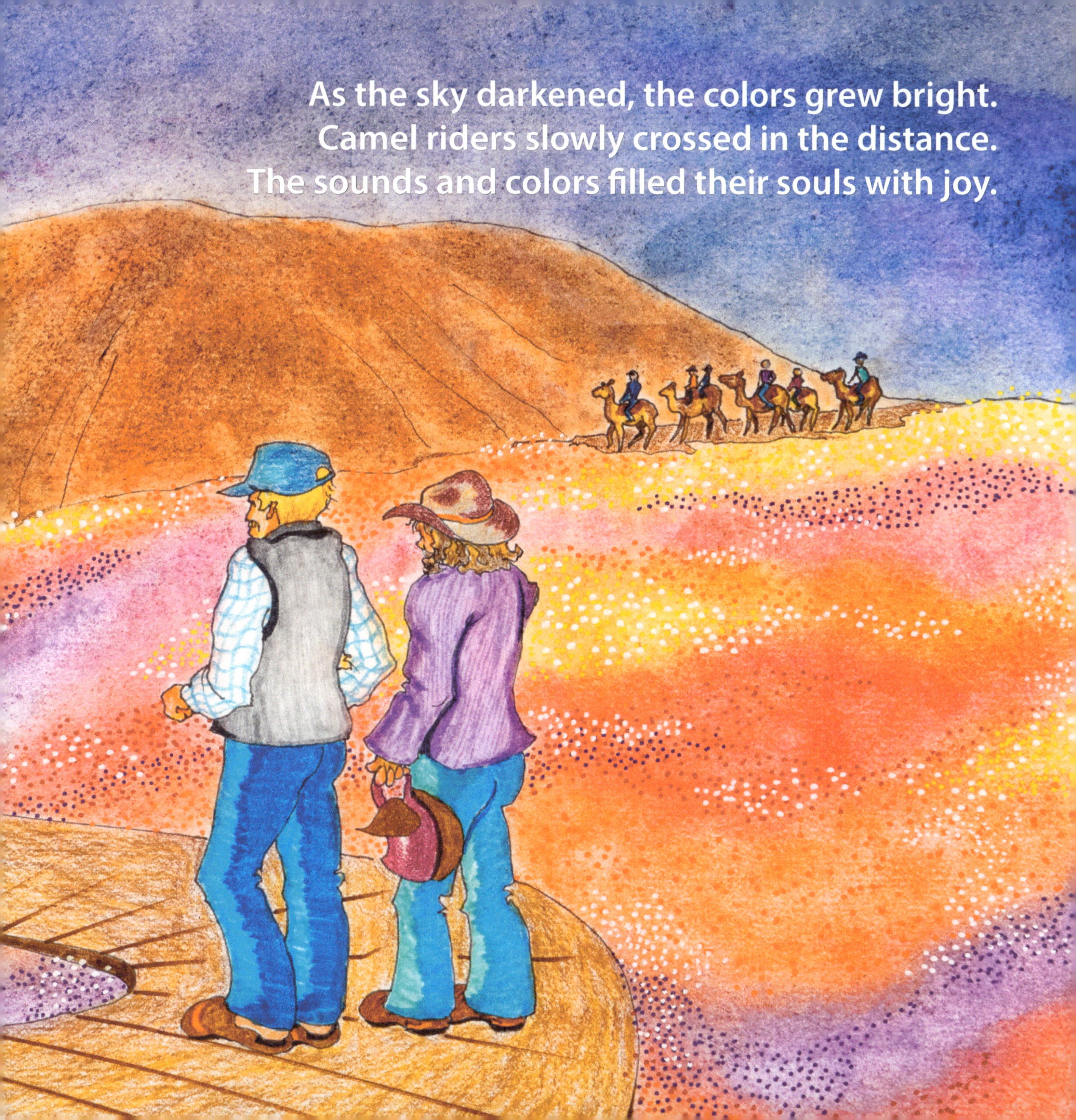

As the sky darkened, the colors grew bright.
Camel riders slowly crossed in the distance.
The sounds and colors filled their souls with joy.

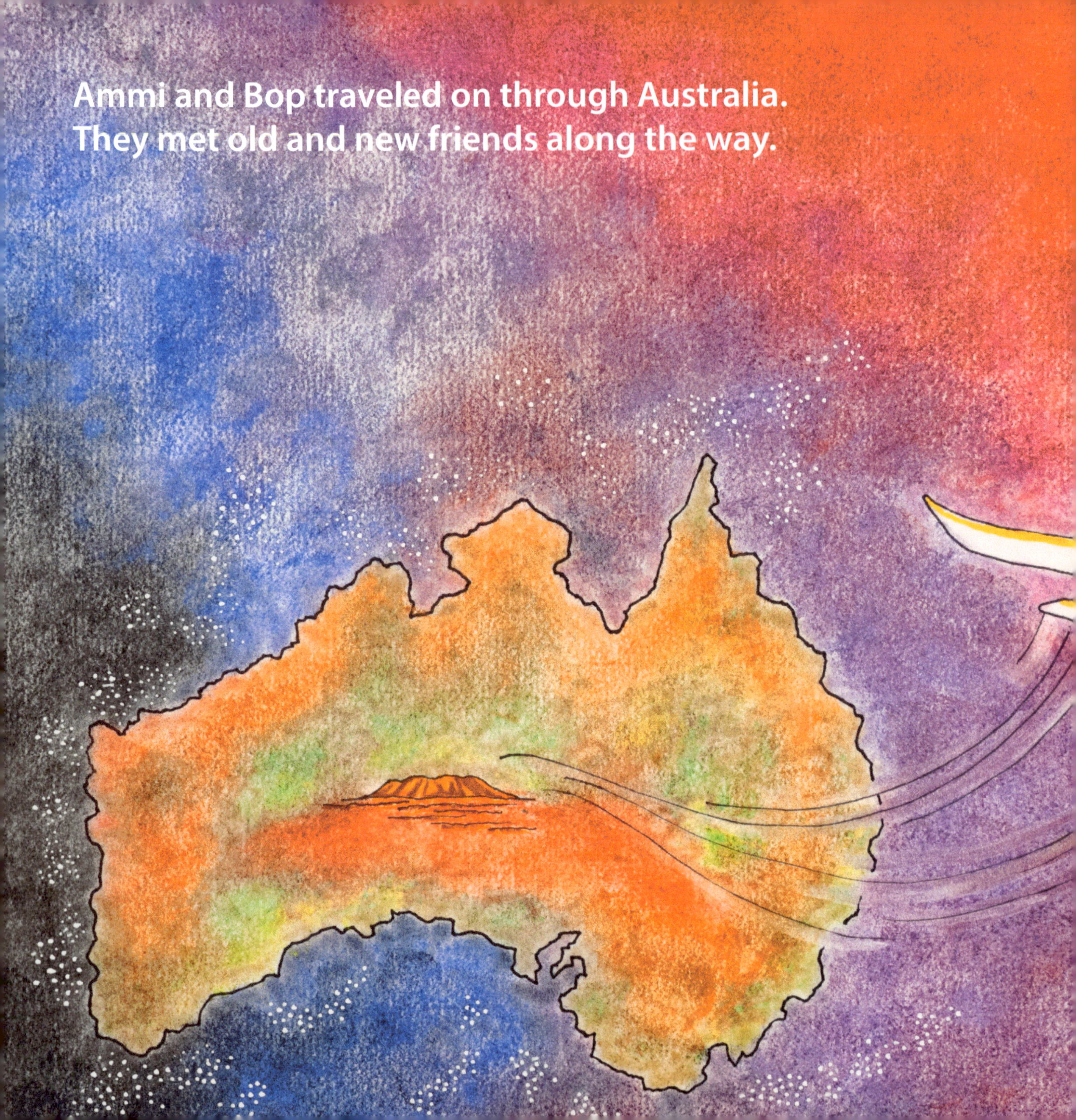

Ammi and Bop traveled on through Australia.
They met old and new friends along the way.

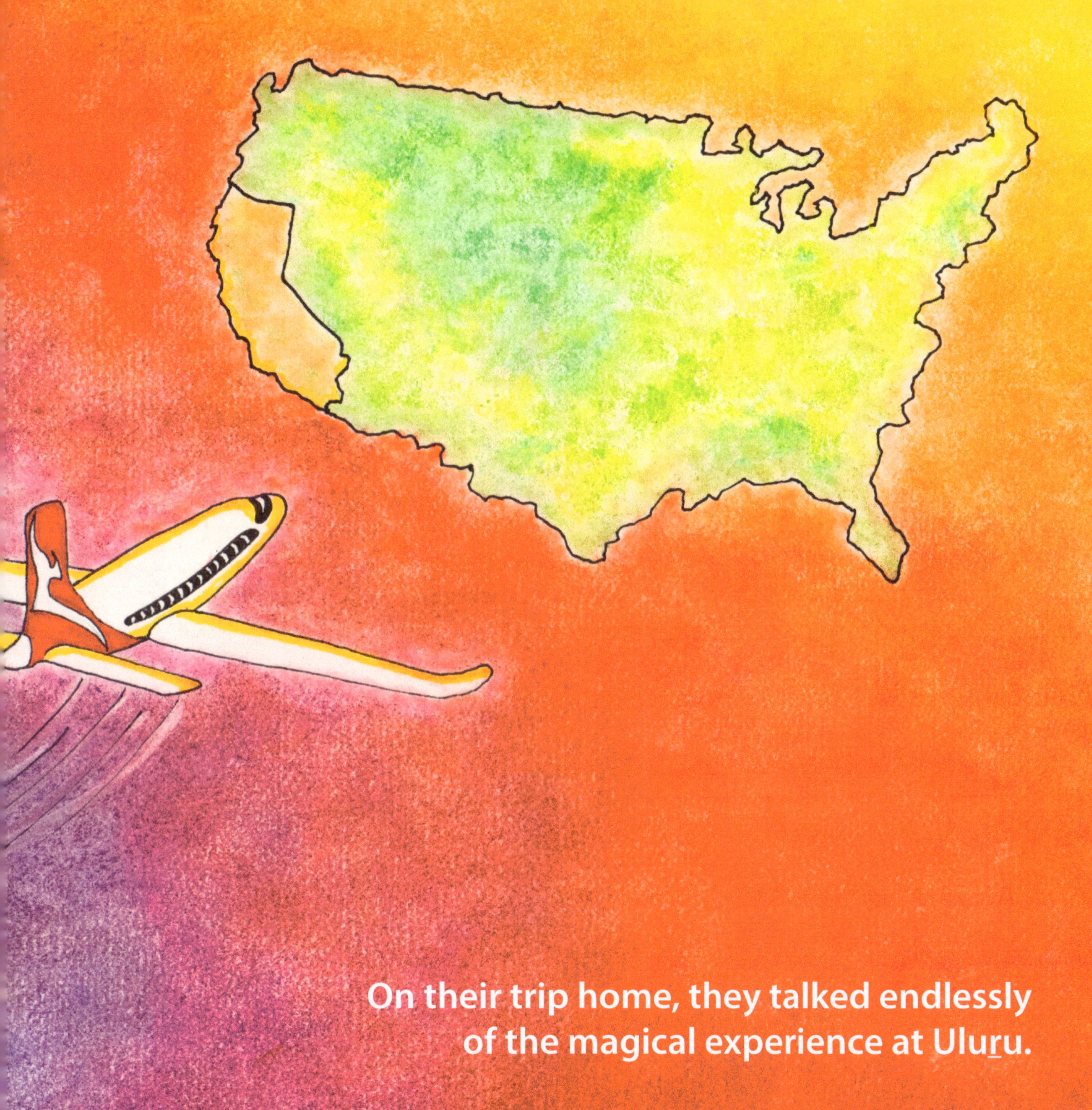

On their trip home, they talked endlessly
of the magical experience at Uluru.

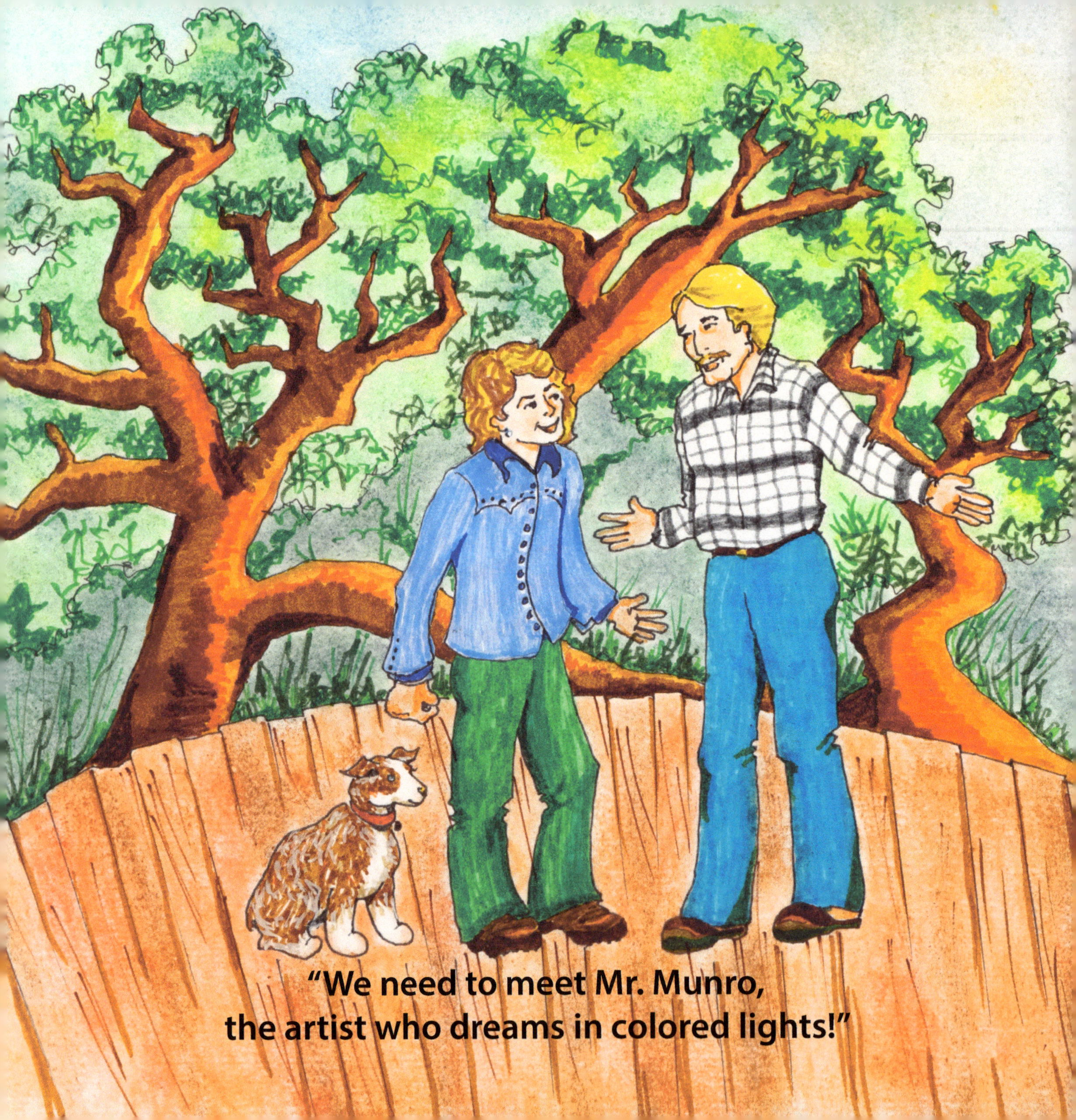
"We need to meet Mr. Munro,
the artist who dreams in colored lights!"

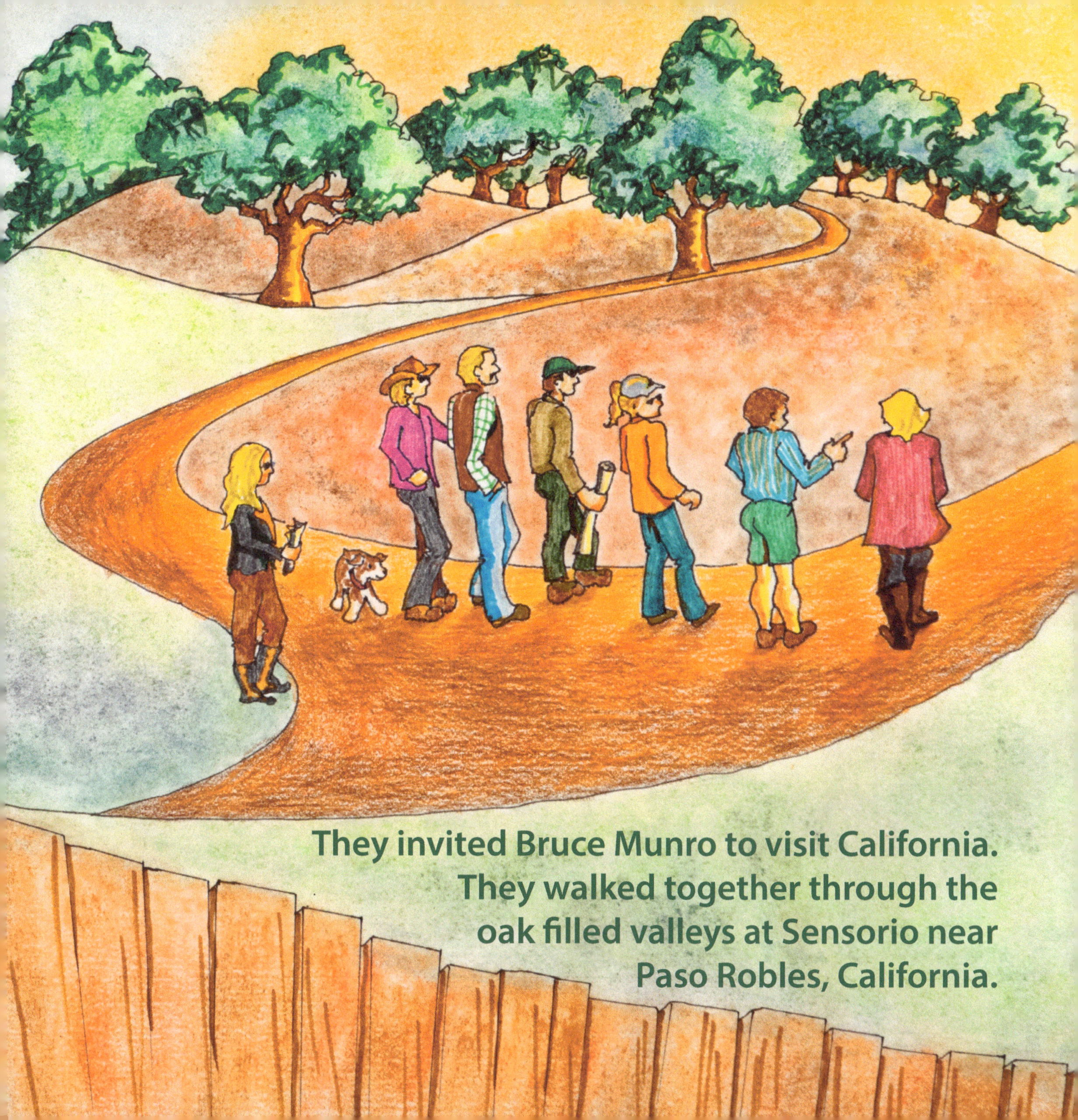

They invited Bruce Munro to visit California.
They walked together through the
oak filled valleys at Sensorio near
Paso Robles, California.

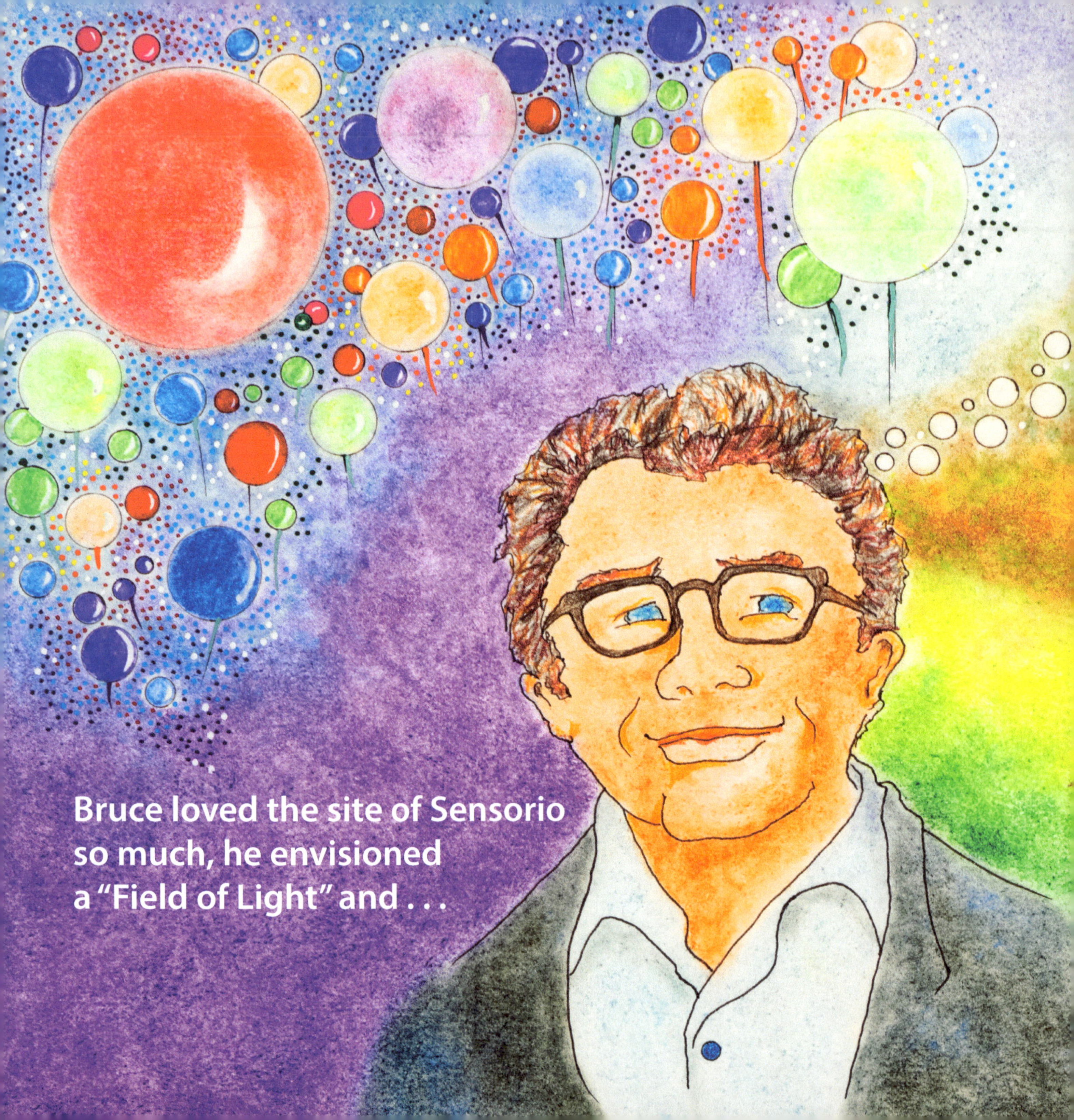
Bruce loved the site of Sensorio
so much, he envisioned
a "Field of Light" and . . .

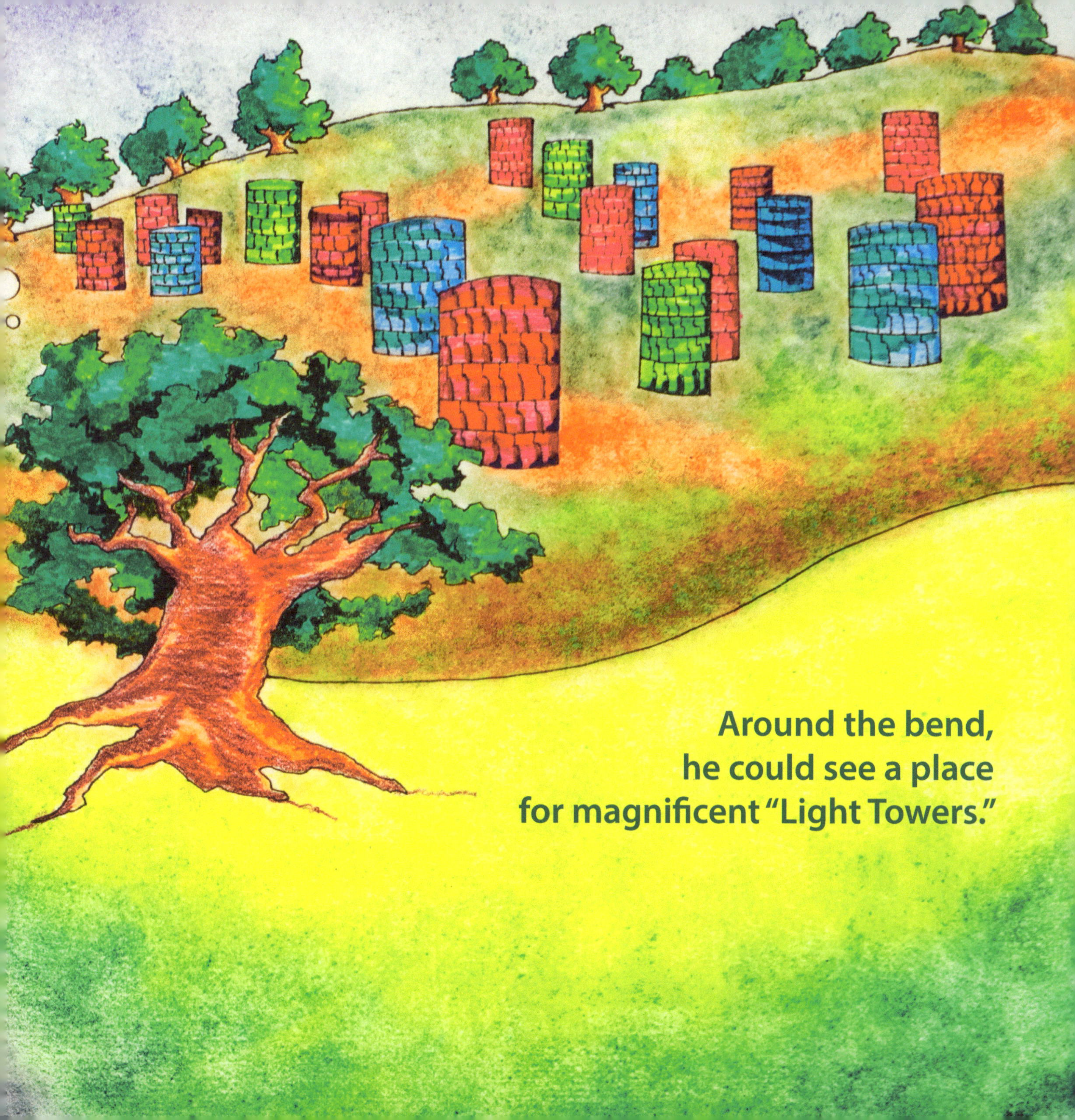

Around the bend,
he could see a place
for magnificent "Light Towers."

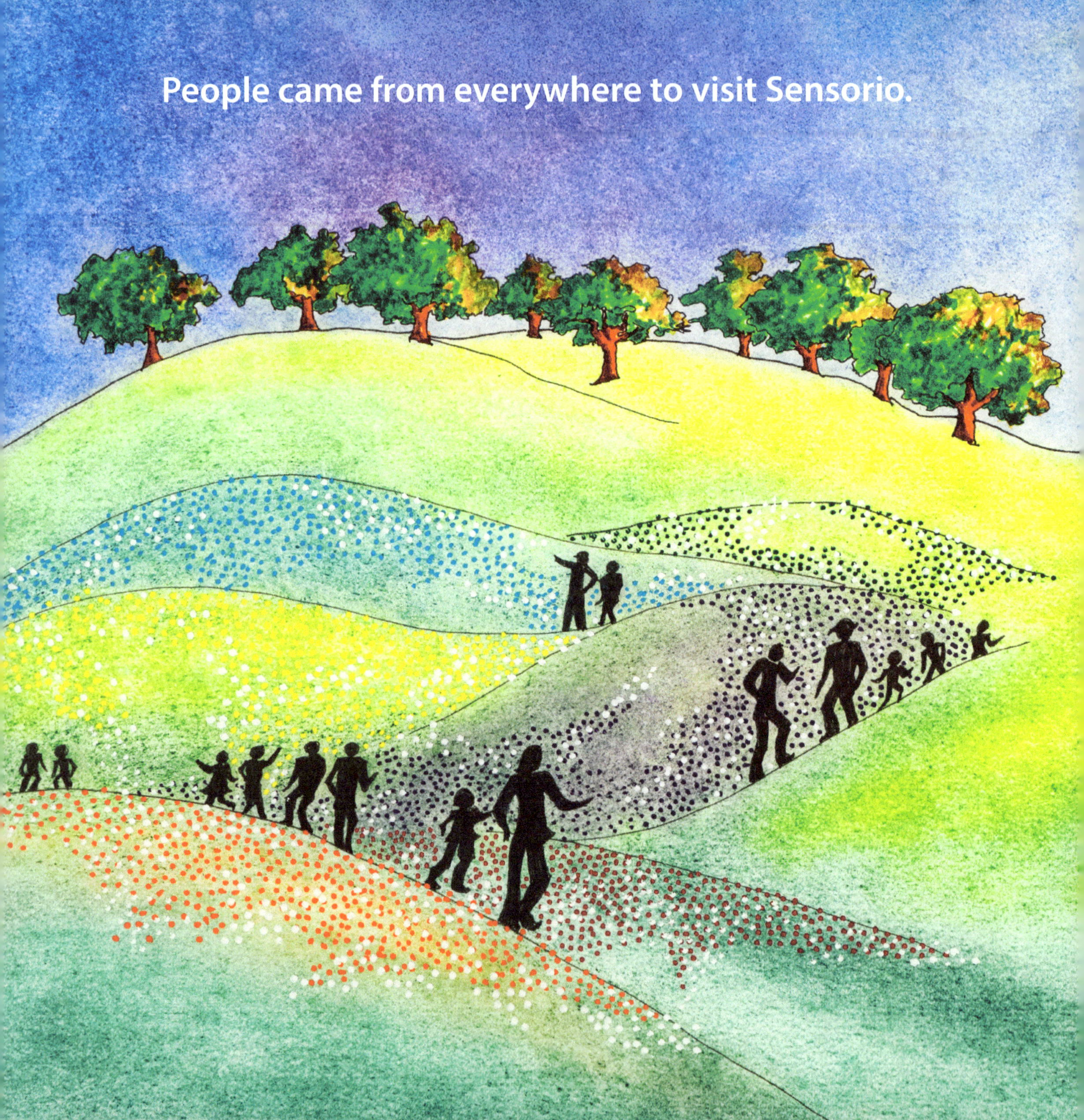
People came from everywhere to visit Sensorio.

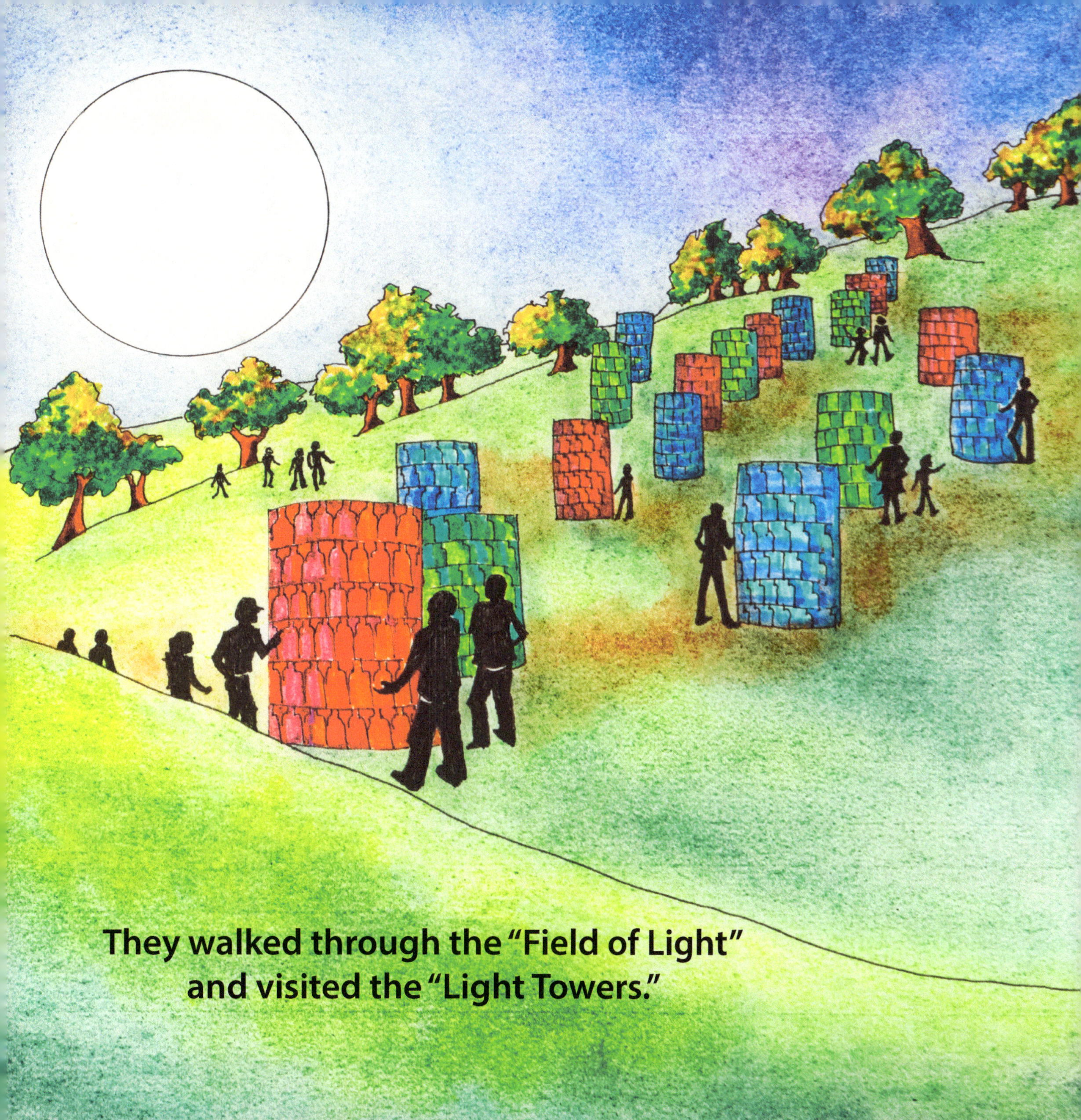

They walked through the "Field of Light"
and visited the "Light Towers."

Ammi and Bop brought back
the best gift of all . . .

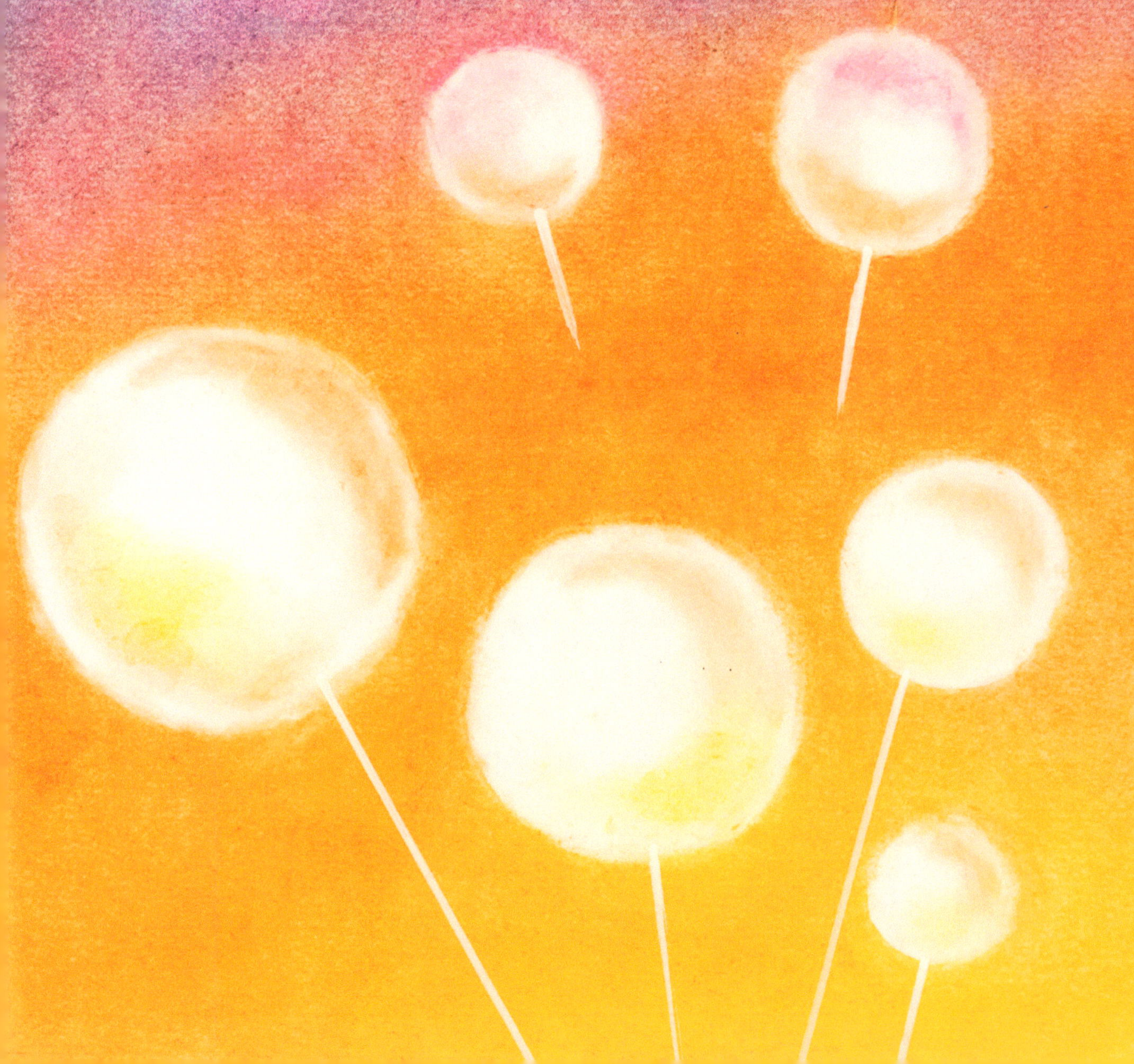
Bruce Munro's
"Field of Light" and "Light Towers" for Sensorio!

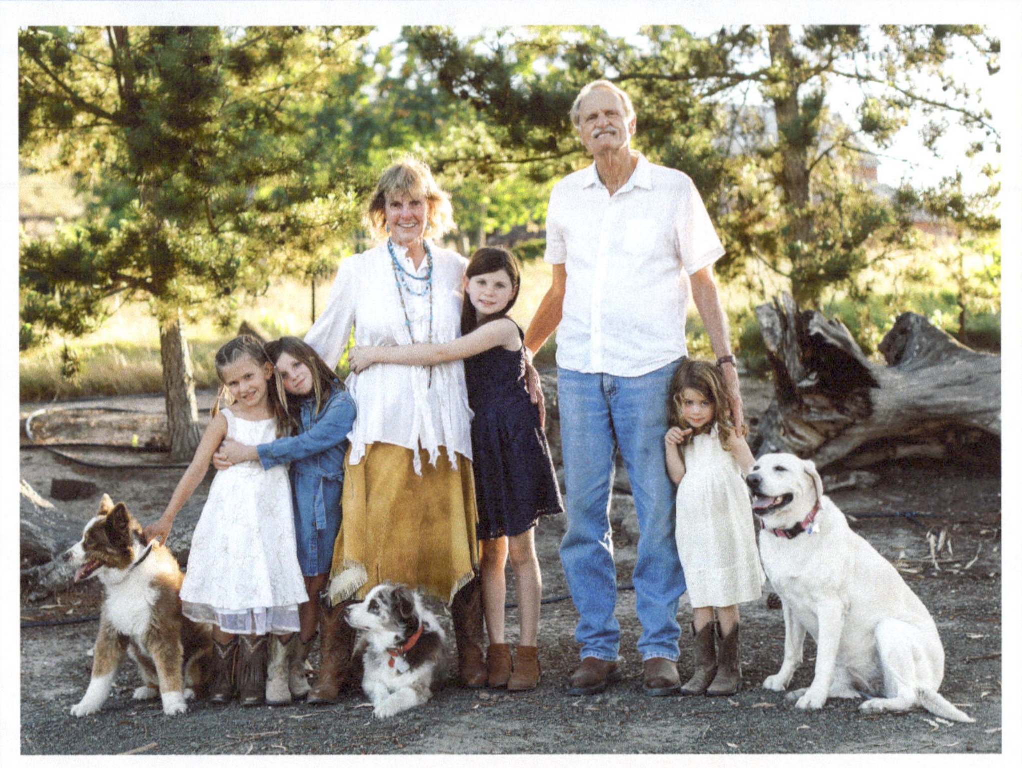

"I love to educate children with fun stories and bright colors!" —Bobbi Dooley Hunter

Bobbi Dooley Hunter

Author/Illustrator Bobbi Dooley Hunter is wife to Ken; mom to Seth and Cameron; mom-in-law to Kara and Sean; Ammi to Ellie, Devyn, Kennedy, Dylan, Emery, Finn, and our beloved pups, Sydney, Bella, Nali, and Cabe. She has written and/or illustrated nine children's books, some published, some in the making!

Sensorio—Finding the Light

Sensorio is a magical land on the central coast of California near the town of Paso Robles. The family created the space with a dream of bringing peace and joy to people who could come and walk through the valleys and hills, experiencing the beauty. When we traveled to Uluru, Australia, and saw Bruce Munro's *Field of Light*, we knew that the luminous experience would be a wonderful complement to the beautiful landscape of Sensorio.